Fact Finders®

The Story of the
American Revolution

The Weapons and Gear of the Revolutionary War

by Graeme Davis

Consultant:
Dennis Showalter
Professor of History
Colorado College
Colorado Springs, Colorado

CAPSTONE PRESS
a capstone imprint

Fact Finders are published by Capstone Press,
1710 Roe Crest Drive, North Mankato, Minnesota 56003.
www.capstonepub.com

Library of Congress Cataloging-in-Publication Data
Davis, Graeme, 1958–
    The weapons and gear of the Revolutionary War / by Graeme Davis.
    p. cm.—(Fact finders. The story of the American Revolution)
    Includes bibliographical references and index.
    Summary: "Describes weapons and gear used in the Revolutionary
War"—Provided by publisher.
    ISBN 978-1-4296-8588-7 (library binding)
    ISBN 978-1-4296-9288-5 (pbk.)
    ISBN 978-1-62065-247-3 (ebook PDF)
    1. United States. Continental Army—Equipment and supplies—Juvenile literature. 2. Military
weapons—United States—History—18th century—Juvenile literature. 3. United States—History—
Revolution, 1775–1783—Juvenile literature. I. Title.
UF523.D385 2013
973.3—dc23   2012001121

Editorial Credits
Jennifer Besel and Megan Peterson, editors; Heidi Thompson, series designer; Kyle Grenz,
    book designer; Wanda Winch, media researcher; Laura Manthe, production specialist

Photo Credits
Alamy: Lebrecht Music and Arts Photo Library, 25, Paul J. Fearn, 16, SuperStock, 26; Armed
Forces History Division/National Museum of American History, Behring Center, Smithsonian
Institution/Karen Carr, artist, 18-19; Bridgeman Art Library International: Peter Newark's
Military Pictures, 17; Capstone: 5; Corbis: Bettmann, 27; Courtesy of Army Art Collection:
U.S. Army Center of Military History, 8 (bottom), 10, 14; Courtesy of the North Carolina
Department of Cultural Resources: Alamance Battleground, 28; Dreamstime: Richard
Gunion, 6; James P. Rowan, 11 (all), 13 (top); Mark Rutledge, 29 (top); National Parks
Service: Colonial National Historical Park, 24; Shutterstock: design36, 22; SuperStock Inc.:
SuperStock, 29 (bottom); www.historicalimagebank.com, 7, 8 (top), 12, 13 (bottom), 15, 23
(all), Painting by Don Troiani, 9, 21

Printed in the United States of America in Brainerd, Minnesota.
032012   006672BANGF12

Table of Contents

CHAPTER 1

Great Britain vs. the Colonies

The year was 1775. Trouble between Great Britain and the American Colonies had been building for years. The British Parliament taxed the colonists to help pay for Great Britain's costly war against France. The colonists had no representation in Parliament and could not object to the taxes. When the colonists complained, Parliament passed harsh laws to punish them. They even sent British troops to keep order.

Finally, on April 19, the trouble erupted into gunfire. Colonists in the Massachusetts Bay Colony clashed with British troops in the towns of Lexington and Concord. The Revolutionary War (1775–1783) had begun. The war dragged on for eight years, killing thousands of American and British soldiers.

From the start, the colonists fought an uphill battle. Great Britain was a major world power. Its army and navy were among the best in the world. British troops were trained to fight using many different weapons.

colonist: someone who lives in a newly settled area

The American colonists had few supplies to build an army and navy. Farmers and craftsmen had already formed small local armies called militias. General George Washington was given the challenge of turning the militias into a professional army. His troops had little training and fewer weapons than the British. Still, they went on to defeat one of the most powerful armies on earth.

CHAPTER 2

Muskets and Rifles

Pop! Pop! Pop! Gunfire exploded as British and American infantries advanced toward each other, shoulder-to-shoulder. Smoke from the gunpowder created a haze over the battlefield. As the soldiers reloaded their muskets, the smoke made it hard to tell the difference between fellow soldiers and the enemy.

Soldiers stood in a line as they fired their muskets at enemy troops.

infantry: a group of soldiers trained to fight and travel on foot

The Brown Bess musket was a common weapon used during the Revolutionary War.

Muskets

Both British and American infantries used muskets as their main weapon. Most of the colonists owned muskets. They used these guns to hunt and to defend against wild animals and other people. Early in the war, the colonists fought with a British musket called the Brown Bess. American gunsmiths patterned their guns after the Brown Bess. Colonists also fought with muskets sent from France.

A musket was a simple gun. It was basically a metal tube that was open at one end. A soldier with a musket could hit a target up to about 50 yards (46 meters) away. Muskets were highly inaccurate at greater distances. They were also slow to reload. A soldier could only fire two or three shots per minute.

FAST FACTS

In the summer of 1776, colonists in New York pulled down a lead statue of Great Britain's King George III. They melted it to make 42,000 musket balls.

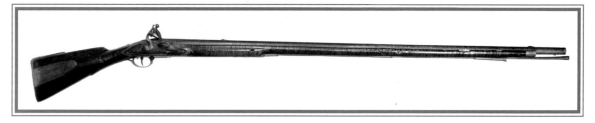

Gunsmiths from Pennsylvania created the Pennsylvania rifle.

Rifles

Soldiers on both sides also fought with rifles. Rifles were mainly used by sharpshooters. Most American sharpshooters were frontiersmen. They were already expert shots before the war started. A sharpshooter could hit a target up to about 400 yards (366 m) away.

According to legend, American sharpshooter Timothy Murphy (top right) shot and killed British general Simon Fraser with a rifle at the Battle of Saratoga.

sharpshooter: someone skilled at hitting small or distant targets

Rifles had spiral grooves on the inside of their barrels, making them more accurate than muskets. The grooves made the ball spin, which helped it fly farther and straighter. The grooves worked only if the ball fit tightly into the barrel. A tight-fitting ball took up to two minutes to reload. In most battles, there was only time to fire a few shots before the enemy charged. That's why most Revolutionary soldiers fought with muskets.

Muzzle Loading

Guns used during the American Revolution were muzzle-loaded. A soldier poured loose gunpowder down the gun's barrel, or muzzle. A piece of cotton or paper wadding was shoved in the barrel to hold the gunpowder in place. Then he dropped the ball into the muzzle and packed everything down using a ramrod. Pulling the trigger snapped a piece of flint against a steel plate. This made a spark, which set the gunpowder on fire and blew the ball out of the gun.

Soldiers used a ramrod to pack the gunpowder and bullet into a gun's muzzle.

CHAPTER 3

Artillery

Large guns, called artillery, were the most powerful weapons used on the battlefields of the American Revolution. Colonists had very few artillery pieces when the war began. They captured these guns from British forces they defeated. These weapons could hit targets up to about 1,800 yards (1.6 kilometers) away.

A field cannon, shown here at the Battle of Trenton in 1776, was easy to move around the battlefield.

Types of Artillery

British and American troops shot three main types of artillery—cannons, mortars, and howitzers. Cannons had long metal barrels. They fired a shot in a straight path. Mortars had shorter, wider barrels than cannons. They fired a shot high in the air, over fort walls. Howitzers could shoot both high in the air and in a straight path.

Some mortars were permanently fixed at high angles to fire shot over the walls of forts.

Artillery in forts and aboard ships sat on carriages with small wheels.

Carriages

Artillery was too large for soldiers to carry. Instead these heavy guns sat on wooden frames called carriages. Cannons in forts and aboard ships sat on low, heavy carriages with four small wheels. A field carriage was much lighter. Its large wheels made a cannon easier to move around a battlefield.

11

Ammunition

It took up to 14 highly trained men to operate a single piece of artillery. Cannons usually fired solid iron balls. Cannonballs weighed from 1 pound (0.5 kilogram) to 24 pounds (11 kg) or more. These heavy balls knocked down the walls of forts. They also bounced along the ground, smashing into enemy troops, horses, and artillery.

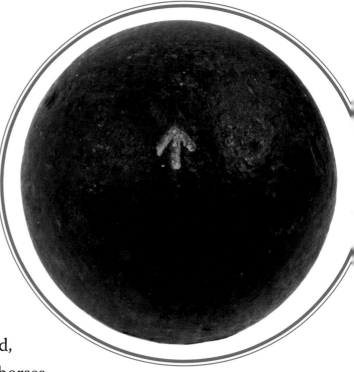

The weight of a cannonball determined which cannon it was fired from. This 12-pound (5.4-kg) cannonball would have been fired from a gun called a 12-pounder.

FAST FACTS

In May 1775, colonels Benedict Arnold and Ethan Allen captured Fort Ticonderoga in New York from the British. American troops took many much-needed cannons from the fort. They used these same cannons to drive the British out of Boston.

Grape shot was made of small balls wrapped in canvas or burlap.

Artillery also fired other kinds of ammunition. Field soldiers packed smaller balls into a fabric or metal wrapping to make grape shot and canister. The wrapping came apart when fired, sending the balls in all directions. Grape shot and canister were deadly at close range and killed many. Soldiers used howitzers and mortars to launch hollow iron balls packed with gunpowder, called shells, over the enemy. When the shells exploded, shrapnel sliced into the troops below.

Cannons aboard ships fired grape shot and chain shot into the masts and rigging of enemy ships. Chain shot consisted of two balls connected by a chain. Ships with damaged masts were slower and easier to defeat.

Chain shot tore apart a ship's masts and rigging.

shrapnel: pieces that have broken off from an explosive shell

13

CHAPTER 4

Close-Combat Weapons

In the 1700s guns were only fired as armies moved toward each other. As the two sides reached each other, soldiers fought hand-to-hand with close-combat weapons.

Soldiers attached bayonets to the barrels of their muskets and attacked enemy troops at close range.

Bayonets

Both British and American infantrymen used bayonets as their main close-combat weapon. The long, metal bayonet blades attached to the barrels of muskets, turning them into spears. Bayonets were fast and easy weapons. A soldier could stab an enemy with a bayonet or hit him with the butt of his gun.

Tomahawks and Hunting Knives

Bayonets could not be attached to rifles. Instead riflemen wielded tomahawks and hunting knives during hand-to-hand combat. A tomahawk was a small ax. They pulled these sharp weapons from their belts as they charged the enemy.

Riflemen fought hand-to-hand combat with tomahawks.

Swords and Sabers

British and American officers used swords in close combat. Officers usually came from wealthy families. They were taught to use swords even before joining the army. The cavalry rode horses into battle and attacked with sabers. These long, steel swords had curved blades about 3 feet (1 m) long.

CHAPTER 5

Ships

At the start of the war, the colonists had no navy. In October 1775 Congress voted to form a Continental navy. This group would face off against the most powerful navy in the world—Great Britain's Royal Navy.

The first American ships were merchant ships converted for war. They were too small to take on Royal Navy warships. Their captains mostly raided British supply ships, cutting off food and equipment for British troops. The Continental navy also hired privateers to attack British cargo ships.

The Continental navy launched the frigate *Confederacy* on November 8, 1778.

privateer: a person who owns a ship licensed to attack enemy ships during wartime

The ships of the American Revolution were wooden sailing ships. Frigates were common ships that sailed during the war. Equipped with at least 24 cannons, these speedy ships acted as scouts and attacked smaller cargo ships. Most frigates had crews of around 200 men. Ships of the line were heavier than frigates. They carried at least 60 cannons. A crew of 600 men or more manned a ship of the line.

The World's First Submarine

American inventor David Bushnell built the world's first combat submarine in 1775. Called the *Turtle*, it was made of oak. The submarine looked like a large walnut and had a one-man crew. A hand-cranked propeller moved it through the water.

The *Turtle* attacked the British HMS *Eagle* close to New York in September 1776. The crewman, Sergeant Ezra Lee, tried to drill into the ship's main body and attach an explosive charge. His drill hit metal and could not get through it. He had to give up. The *Turtle* never completed a successful mission.

The *Turtle* (bottom right) was the world's first combat submarine.

CHAPTER 6

Uniforms

Can you imagine wearing the same clothing for months or even years at a time? Soldiers in the Continental army often had to do just that. Congress could not afford to provide uniforms to every soldier. Supply lines carrying new uniforms weren't able to catch up with all the troops. Many soldiers fought in their own clothes.

Shoes and Boots

Soldiers in the American Revolution walked wherever they went. Keeping their feet dry, warm, and protected was important. Continental soldiers without shoes wore rags on their feet, even in winter.

Many British and American troops wore tricorn hats during the war.

British grenadiers could be recognized by their tall bearskin hats.

Soldiers fortunate enough to own footwear wore leather shoes. Two pieces of leather were wrapped around the foot and secured with a buckle. During this time period, there weren't right and left shoes. The men wore their shoes on different feet each day to avoid wearing them out as quickly. The cavalry and some officers wore leather boots. The boots protected their legs while on horseback.

Hats and Helmets

British and American soldiers wore similar headgear. The three-sided tricorn hat was common during the war. Troops also wore cocked hats, with the brim turned up on only two sides. A turned-up brim made it more difficult for the hat to be blown off by the wind. Officers wore feathers in their hats. British grenadier soldiers wore tall hats made of bearskin.

When charging into battle with swords drawn, the British and American cavalry needed protection for their heads. They wore helmets made of hard leather or brass. Some were covered with bear fur or horse hair to fend off sword blows.

Coats and Shirts

Most units of the British Army wore red coats. British troops were sometimes called Redcoats or lobster backs. The Continental army wasn't dressed as uniformly as the British. Each militia wore its own uniform. In 1779 General Washington ordered that soldiers wear blue coats made of wool. Different colors on the coats' facings showed which state a soldier came from.

Uniform Facings of the Continental Army

Red facings: Pennsylvania, Delaware, Maryland, and Virginia

White facings: New Hampshire, Massachusetts, Rhode Island, and Connecticut

Blue facings: buttonholes edged with white tape: North Carolina, South Carolina, and Georgia

Buff facings: New York and New Jersey

facing: the lining at the edge of a garment or around a buttonhole

Not all Continental soldiers had uniform coats. Instead they wore hunting shirts. Made of linen or deerskin, these loose shirts were easy for soldiers to move in. The shirts were dyed different colors for each regiment, such as yellow, blue, green, purple, brown, black, or white. The hunting shirt was often the only uniform a soldier owned.

Some hunting shirts were pullovers. Others were open down the front.

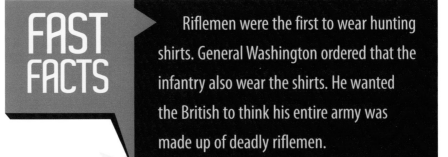

FAST FACTS

Riflemen were the first to wear hunting shirts. General Washington ordered that the infantry also wear the shirts. He wanted the British to think his entire army was made up of deadly riflemen.

21

Food and Rations

Soldiers in the American Revolution wanted to set up camp near cities or towns. Daily food rations near cities often included beef, pork, fish, rice, potatoes, peas, and even fresh bread.

Soldiers on the march didn't fare as well. It was difficult to bring food to an army spread out in the wilderness. Starving Continental soldiers often ate "fire cakes." They mixed water and flour together and cooked the paste over a fire.

Both the British and Continental armies attacked each other's supply lines to get extra food for their own starving troops. Most British and American soldiers never received their full rations. They often went hungry. Because the colonists controlled the countryside, the British could not find food locally. Most of the food they ate had to be shipped from Great Britain.

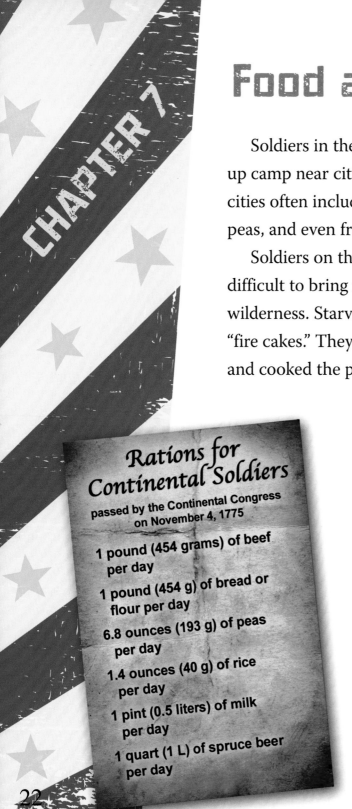

Rations for Continental Soldiers
passed by the Continental Congress on November 4, 1775

1 pound (454 grams) of beef per day

1 pound (454 g) of bread or flour per day

6.8 ounces (193 g) of peas per day

1.4 ounces (40 g) of rice per day

1 pint (0.5 liters) of milk per day

1 quart (1 L) of spruce beer per day

Lack of fresh fruits and vegetables did more than make soldiers hungry. Troops on both sides became sick with scurvy. Congress added spruce beer to the Continental soldiers' rations. It contained vitamin C, which helped prevent the disease. The beer was made from spruce tree needles.

Soldiers wore haversacks slung over one shoulder.

Haversacks and Canteens

Soldiers carried their food rations and water in haversacks and canteens. A haversack was a bag made of canvas or linen. Some British haversacks were made of goatskin. Soldiers drank water from canteens made of wood or metal. Sometimes several soldiers had to drink from the same canteen.

The American canteen shown here is made of wood.

CHAPTER 8

Shelter

During the American Revolution, soldiers had to march in the rain, heat, cold, and even snow. They set up camps in all kinds of weather. Army camps could be disgusting, dangerous places. They often smelled of sweat, dirt, and human waste. Soldiers sometimes froze to death during the winter.

Tents

An army on the march slept in tents. Made of canvas, most tents were 6.5 feet (2 m) square. They were built for six men but often housed more. Soldiers slept on the ground, with only blankets to keep them warm. Some men had to sleep out in the open. They made crude shelters out of sticks and blankets.

George Washington (center), shown here at Yorktown, set up his headquarters in tents while on the march.

Huts

FAST FACTS

In 1775 Continental soldiers were housed at Harvard University in Cambridge, Massachusetts.

The cold and snow made fighting difficult. The British and Continental armies usually didn't fight during the winter. They spent the winter in more permanent camps. In the winter of 1777–1778, General Washington's army set up camp at Valley Forge in Pennsylvania. His men built around 2,000 log huts. Soldiers' huts were 14 feet (4.3 m) by 16 feet (4.9 m) and held up to 12 men. They slept on wooden bunks inside the hut. The men piled leaves or straw on the bunks to make them more comfortable. Huts offered more protection than tents but were still drafty and cold.

Continental soldiers at Valley Forge built log huts before the brutal winter of 1777–1778.

25

CHAPTER 9

Disease and Doctors

Revolutionary soldiers were in constant danger, both on and off the battlefield. More soldiers died of illness than battle wounds. Doctors during this period had very little knowledge of how the body works. Still, they did their best to save lives.

Doctors treated wounded soldiers at the Battle of Bunker Hill in 1775, the war's bloodiest battle.

Hospitals

Continental camp hospitals were cramped, disease-filled places. Sick and wounded soldiers shared small rooms with little fresh air. Dirty clothing and bedding went unchanged. Germs passed from soldier to soldier. The men suffered from diseases such as smallpox. Smaller, less crowded hospitals were set up later in the war.

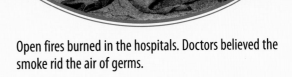

Open fires burned in the hospitals. Doctors believed the smoke rid the air of germs.

Sick and wounded British soldiers were a little better off than the Americans. British doctors understood the dangers of cramped hospitals and preferred smaller hospitals. The British also controlled the import of medical supplies.

smallpox: a disease that spreads easily from person to person, causing chills, fever, pimples that scar, and even death

Medicine

Medicine and other supplies were kept in medical chests. Doctors commonly used medicine to make patients vomit or have diarrhea. Doctors at that time believed they could force disease out of the body. The British blocked the east coast, stopping imports of medicine as well as other goods. American doctors often had trouble finding medicine.

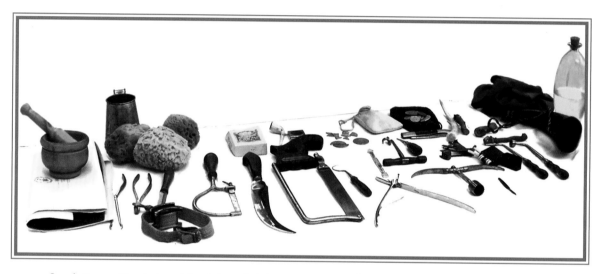

Revolutionary War doctors did not clean their instruments properly after performing surgeries.

Surgery

Surgery during the Revolutionary War was gruesome. Surgeons used knives, drills, and forceps to amputate wounded limbs and remove musket balls. Pain medication did not exist. During surgery soldiers chewed on lead bullets to keep from screaming or biting their tongues. Doctors did not know about germs. They did not sterilize their instruments. Patients often became infected or went into shock.

amputate: to cut off someone's arm, leg, or other body part, usually because the part is damaged

sterilize: to clean something so thoroughly that no germs or dirt remain

Soldiers chewed on lead bullets during surgery to help deal with the pain.

Bloodletting was another common surgery performed on sick and wounded troops. Doctors used small knives called lancets to cut into soldiers' veins and remove "bad blood." They believed patients would quickly regrow healthy blood. Removing blood from sick soldiers usually made their conditions worse. Some even died.

The End of the War

When American forces defeated the British at Yorktown in 1781, the British realized they could not win the war. They had serious supply problems, and it was expensive to keep so many troops in America. The United States became an independent, free nation. It was built by colonists armed with muskets and bayonets.

The British surrendered at Yorktown on October 19, 1781.

Glossary

amputate (AM-pyuh-tayt)—to cut off someone's arm, leg, or other body part, usually because the part is damaged

colonist (KAH-luh-nist)—someone who lives in a newly settled area

facing (FAYSS-ing)—the lining at the edge of a garment or around a buttonhole

infantry (IN-fuhn-tree)—a group of soldiers trained to fight and travel on foot

privateer (prye-vuh-TEER)—a person who owns a ship licensed to attack enemy ships during wartime

scurvy (SKUR-vee)—a deadly disease caused by lack of vitamin C; scurvy produces swollen limbs, bleeding gums, and weakness

sharpshooter (SHARP-shoo-tur)—someone skilled at hitting small or distant targets

shrapnel (SHRAP-nuhl)—pieces that have broken off from an explosive shell

smallpox (SMAWL-poks)—a disease that spreads easily from person to person, causing chills, fever, pimples that scar, and even death

sterilize (STER-uh-lize)—to clean something so thoroughly that no germs or dirt remain

Read More

Burgan, Michael. *Weapons, Gear, and Uniforms of the American Revolution.* Equipped for Battle. Mankato, Minn.: Capstone Press, 2012.

Jeffrey, Gary. *George Washington and the Winter at Valley Forge.* Graphic Heroes of the American Revolution. New York: Gareth Stevens Pub., 2011.

Raum, Elizabeth. *The Cold, Hard Facts about Science and Medicine in Colonial America.* Life in the American Colonies. Mankato, Minn.: Capstone Press, 2012.

Internet Sites

FactHound offers a safe, fun way to find Internet sites related to this book. All of the sites on FactHound have been researched by our staff.

Here's all you do:

Visit *www.facthound.com*

Type in this code: 9781429685887

Check out projects, games and lots more at
www.capstonekids.com

Index